Edward a_____:

Prince and Pauper

Sarah Fleming

OXFORD

UNIVERSITY PRESS

OXFORD
UNIVERSITY PRESS

Great Clarendon Street, Oxford OX2 6DP

Oxford University Press is a department of the University of Oxford.
It furthers the University's objective of excellence in research, scholarship,
and education by publishing worldwide in

Oxford   New York

Auckland   Cape Town   Dar es Salaam   Hong Kong   Karachi
Kuala Lumpur   Madrid   Melbourne   Mexico City   Nairobi
New Delhi   Shanghai   Taipei   Toronto

With offices in

Argentina   Austria   Brazil   Chile   Czech Republic   France   Greece
Guatemala   Hungary   Italy   Japan   Poland   Portugal   Singapore
South Korea   Switzerland   Thailand   Turkey   Ukraine   Vietnam

Oxford is a registered trade mark of Oxford University Press
in the UK and in certain other countries

British Library Cataloguing in Publication Data

Data available

ISBN 978-0-19-919848-1

17 19 20 18 16

Printed in China by Imago

Paper used in the production of this book is a natural,
recyclable product made from wood grown in sustainable forests.
The manufacturing process conforms to the environmental
regulations of the country of origin.

Acknowledgements

The publisher would like to thank the following for permission to reproduce
photographs: p4/5t&b Ronald Grant Archive; p6/7 The Royal Collection © 2004, Her Majesty
Queen Elizabeth II; p9 Mary Evans Picture Library; p20&23 Erich Lessing/AKG–Images

Illustrations by KJA-Artists.com

The publisher would like to thank Penguin Books Ltd for permission to reproduce
the cover of *The Prince and the Pauper* by Mark Twain (Penguin Classics, 2004)

Contents

The Prince and the Pauper

Mark Twain's fiction book

The story is set in Tudor England at the end of Henry VIII's **reign**. It is about Henry's son, Edward, and a beggar boy, Tom, who looked exactly like him. Mark Twain, an American writer, wrote about what happened when the poor boy – a **pauper** – and the prince changed places.

The plot of the book describes how the boys each discover a completely different England that they didn't know about.

❖ Prince Edward discovers what it is like to be poor.

❖ Pauper Tom discovers what it is like to be a prince.

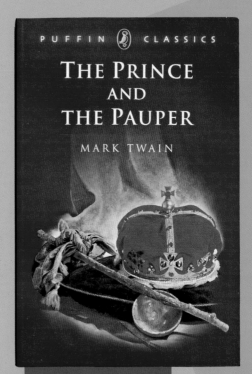

PUFFIN CLASSICS

THE PRINCE AND THE PAUPER

MARK TWAIN

Mark Twain wrote this book in 1881.

This fact book

'Edward and Tom' is about the kinds of lives that these two would have had in real life.

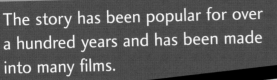

The story has been popular for over a hundred years and has been made into many films.

presents MARK TWAIN'S immortal romance "The Prince & The Pauper"

5

The families

Mark Twain's story begins like this:-

'In the ancient city of London, on a certain autumn day in the second quarter of the sixteenth century, a boy was born to a poor family of the name of Canty, who did not want him. On the same day another English child was born to a rich family of the name of Tudor, who did want him.'

Why did the Canty family not want a child?

The Cantys were beggars. Another child was another mouth to feed.

Rich landowners were throwing people off their farms in the countryside. These people came to the towns to look for work, but there were not enough jobs. So they became beggars, pleading with people for money on the streets.

It was against the law to beg in Tudor times, so Tom's family had to be very careful.

This portrait shows Henry VIII with his arm around Edward. Next to him is his third wife, Jane Seymour. She was Edward's mother, but had actually died shortly after giving birth to him. On the left of the portrait is Henry's daughter Mary Tudor, and on the right, his daughter Elizabeth.

Why did the Tudor family want a boy?

The Tudor family is King Henry VIII's family. Henry Tudor wanted a son to become the next King of England after him. He wanted a male **heir** because women were looked down on then (though his daughter Elizabeth I was very successful!). Neither of Henry VIII's first two wives had baby boys who survived.

Beggars could be put in stocks, whipped, or have their tongues cut out.

FICTION

Pauper Tom

Although Tom is a fictional character, his life is an example of a real beggar boy's life in Tudor London.

Father:	John Canty (thief)
Mother:	Mrs Canty (beggar)
Sisters:	Bet & Nan (twins, 6 years older)

TOM

born
12 October 1537

Swapped places

Swapped back
Became rich

Died
An old man

born
12 October 1537

Swapped places

Became King
28 Jan 1547, age 9
Swapped back

Died
6 July 1553, age 15

FACT

Prince Edward

Edward was the King's beloved son, his pride and joy. Anything Edward wanted he could have. He was brought up as the future king, with an education to match. He lived in castles and palaces in the company of the **court**. He became king when he was only 9.

Father:	Henry VIII
Mother:	Jane Seymour (Henry's 3rd wife).
Sisters:	Mary (half-sister, 21 years older)
	Elizabeth (half-sister, 4 years older)

A king's court was the group of richest and noblest gentlemen and ladies of the country who used to go and stay with the royal family and keep them company.

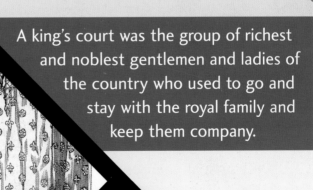

House and home

Prince

Edward had more homes and belongings than he probably ever saw. In the summer there was often **plague** and disease in London, so Edward would go with his father to one of their palaces in the country. For the hunting season he might go to Hampton Court where there was a deer park. He liked to have Christmas in Greenwich.

He was dressed by servants in clean clothes everyday, sometimes changing for dinner. He wore the finest materials, brought from all around the known world.

Pauper

Tom lived with his family in one rented room. He slept on old straw on the floor, with his sisters and his grandmother. His parents had a bed. They owned very little, and rarely had enough money to make a fire.

Tom had one set of ragged clothes, which were only washed when he played in the river.

Food

Most food in Tudor England was grown in England. People ate bread and English vegetables, but they did not have rice, or pasta. Potatoes were not introduced to England until Elizabeth I's reign (1558–1603).

Any food that was brought into England was very expensive. Spices and foods like oranges, were only eaten by the rich.

They really did make pies with live birds inside!

The Tudors ate a lot more meat than we do, and they ate parts of the animal that we don't eat very often these days: tongue, heart, brain, liver.

Everyone, including children, drank mead – beer made from honey – and ale.

Pauper

When Tom got money from begging, he would buy himself a pie or some bread. Sometimes his mother would save him a crust and go hungry herself. Sometimes he would go hungry for days. His poor **diet** would stop him growing properly, making him weak and sickly.

Prince

Edward ate very well. Ale and bread for breakfast, a main 'dinner' in the middle of the day, and a supper in the evening. On feast days, dinner could last all day.

Education

Prince

Edward's education started when he was three years old. By the time he was six, Edward could read Greek and Latin well.

Prince Edward's whipping boy

Whipping boy

In Tudor times pupils who did bad work were whipped. But because he was a prince, Edward could not be hurt. So he had a 'whipping boy,' Barnaby Fitzpatrick. If Edward did badly in his lessons, Barnaby was smacked. (Luckily Edward was a good pupil and they became best friends!)

The Prince's diary

Diary

Edward wrote a diary.

Pauper

Most paupers could not read – most never even went to school. Tom was taught to read by a priest who lived in his building. He had very few books to read from, and no paper to write on.

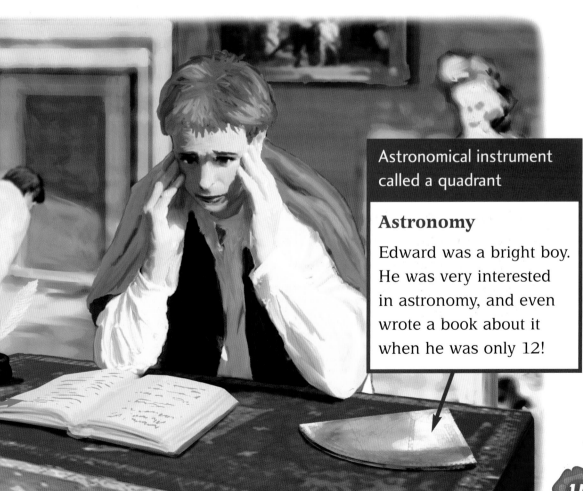

Astronomical instrument called a quadrant

Astronomy

Edward was a bright boy. He was very interested in astronomy, and even wrote a book about it when he was only 12!

Prince

Edward liked football. For him, this would be one of many pastimes.

Pauper

For Tom, watching football would be one of the highlights of his year.

Tudor football: the rules:

* ❖ The goal posts are set more than a kilometre apart.
* ❖ No lines, or fixed size to the 'field' (which was often a whole village!).
* ❖ Any number of players on each side.
* ❖ Kick, pick up the ball and throw it.

(Scoring goals was about the only thing there still is in common with today's game!)

This is what someone writing in the 16th Century said about football:

from: Philip Stubbs, *The Anatomy of Abuses* (1585)

'Football is more a fight than a game... Sometimes their necks are broken, sometimes their backs, sometimes their legs... Football encourages envy and hatred... sometimes fighting, murder and a great loss of blood.'

Tournaments were held to celebrate big events like weddings or visits from important people. Tournaments began in medieval times, when knights fought each other to the death. Tudor tournaments were more about acting and having fun.

People from the Court played at being medieval knights. Often the whole tournament was based round a story and people acted parts such as 'The Black Knight'.

Prince

The prince was guest of honour, and had the best seat.

Tudor jousting

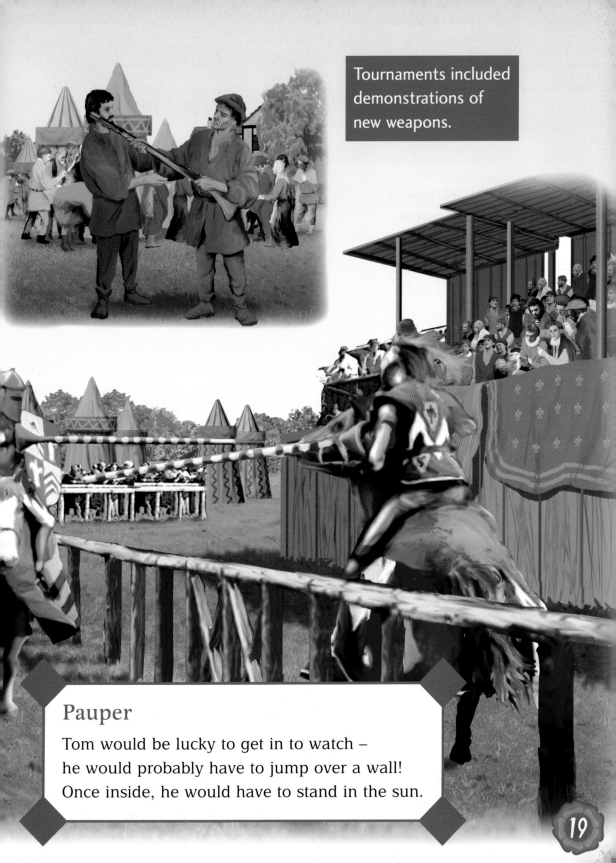

Tournaments included demonstrations of new weapons.

Pauper

Tom would be lucky to get in to watch – he would probably have to jump over a wall! Once inside, he would have to stand in the sun.

King Edward VI

Edward was only nine when he became king. An uncle helped him rule.

Edward made some laws to make ruling the country easier.

He changed old laws to make religion simpler. Church services were said in English – not Latin – for the first time, so that everyone could understand them. He made a prayer book in English too.

Edward being crowned

Execution of the Duke of Somerset

During his reign, Edward had several people **beheaded**, including two of his own uncles! When one, the Duke of Somerset, was **executed**, Edward coldly wrote in his diary:-

'Jan 22. 1552

The Duke of Somerset had his head cut off upon Tower Hill between eight and nine o'clock in the morning.'

Pauper

For paupers, executions were a good day out. There was a jolly crowd atmosphere, street food sellers, begging was good and there were lots of pockets to steal from too.

Religion and heresy

Although Edward had some people executed, his reign was far less bloody than those of most **monarchs** in countries in Europe at that time, including England.

Look at this table, which shows the number of people executed for **heresy** during three reigns in England. At this time people were accused of heresy if they refused to follow the same religion as the reigning monarch.

Monarch	Dates	Burnt for heresy
Henry VIII	1509–1547	81
Edward VI	1547–1553	2
Mary	1553–1558	280

In his book, Mark Twain suggests that Edward ordered few executions because he knew what it was like to be poor due to swapping places with Tom.

People were burned to death for heresy. The burnings took place in public, usually on market day so that as many people as possible would see the executions.

The End

Edward's death

Edward could have become a good king, but he was never very healthy. He died when he was only 15, without an heir.

His eldest half-sister, Mary, became Queen after Edward's death.

And what of Tom?

In the fictional story, everything ends happily. Edward becomes the King of England. He gives Tom, and his family, a home in a charity hospital. Tom lives 'to be a very old man, a handsome, white-haired old fellow.' But in reality, this was most unlikely to have happened. Paupers often died quite young, suffering from disease and hunger.

The fictional Tom as an old man and governor of Christ's Hospital

Index

Glossary

behead – to chop someone's head off, to execute

court – the people chosen to be in the King's company or retinue

diet – kinds of meals eaten to keep healthy

execute – to kill as a punishment

fact – something we know is true

fiction – an imagined story

heir – a person who is in direct line to inherit the crown or a special position

heresy – when people refused to believe in the same religion as the monarch

monarch – a ruler who is a king or queen, emperor or empress

pauper – someone who had no money to live off

plague – a dangerous illness that spreads very quickly

reign – time being king or queen